THE
Archive Photographs
SERIES

KINGSTON UPON HULL

THE
Archive Photographs
SERIES

KINGSTON UPON HULL

Compiled by
Ben and Mave Chapman

CHALFORD

First published 1996
Copyright © Ben and Mave Chapman, 1996

The Chalford Publishing Company
St Mary's Mill, Chalford,
Stroud, Gloucestershire, GL6 8NX

ISBN 0 7524 0663 9

Typesetting and origination by
The Chalford Publishing Company
Printed in Great Britain by
Redwood Books, Trowbridge

Dedication

For the late Nora and Charles Stocker Chapman
who had childhood memories of the First World War and
who unflinchingly braved the horrors of the Hull blitz of the Second World War.
Despite this, Chas and Nora brought up their three children with love
and kindness, tempered with a strong sense of moral duty.

Contents

Acknowledgements

First our grateful thanks go to Mr Norman Ellis for kindly loaning us a number of rare postcards from his collection, which have made this book possible; to Mr Ron Grayson of Bilton who generously allowed us to select items from his collection and Mrs Wendy Graves of Withernsea who also loaned material. Thanks also to our neice and chauffeur Jane Conroy for conveying us, often at short notice, to various postcard fairs around the country and to our dear friend Wayne Wolton, who is always there with a smile and advice when he is most needed to keep up our morale. We also acknowledge the facilities offered by the Hull Local History Library and the Withernsea Town Library.

Ben and Mave Chapman
September 1996

Introduction

The city of Kingston upon Hull has a very long and distinguished history. In 1993 it celebrated the seven hundredth anniversary of the purchase of the town by King Edward I from the Abbot of Meaux and, in his first Royal Charter it was proclaimed as the King's Town. Thus it became known as Kingston upon Hull but over the years it was more generally referred to simply as Hull. With the inception of the recent boundary changes the city has once more reverted to the more dignified and correct designation of Kingston upon Hull.

There have been numerous books written recording the history of this very important and commercially successful port. Two of the books from the last century which are frequently consulted and accepted as authoratitive are the scholarly works of Sheahan and T. Tindall Wildridge, who not only writes about Hull and some of its prominent citizens but also illustrates the works with his own meritorious drawings.

There have, of course, been later scholarly histories of the city, each with the author's own interpretation. In more recent years a number of picture books of varying merit have been produced, some from specialist angles and others simply showing the city streets of bygone days. For this particular volume the authors have taken as their theme the word from the back cover, 'nostalgia', and have chosen to portray life in the city over a certain period. They have concentrated on events which often had far reaching effects or were merely interesting minor local occurrences. To pursue this theme the authors have, of necessity, included some pictures of street scenes in order to convey the atmosphere of the period and, in some cases, the changing scene. They have not only chosen city centre streets but also others with an interesting history of the development.

The role of the church has been considered, with the exception of Holy Trinity which of course dominates the city and has been well documented. There are places of entertainment and some of the entertainers who gave so much enjoyment in those laid-back days. Parades and events all fill the rich tapestry of city life; the advantage with some of these occasions was the presence of a band and other items of interest, perhaps decorated floats or a person of note. Such occasions were a great source of pleasure to many of the poorer members of the community who could not, perhaps, afford the coppers which were charged for most functions, amateur concerts and the like.

The book touches on adversity such as the Zeppelin raids of the First World War, some of the tragedies which had their profound effect on the city and of course, the fate of the 'Pals' Battalions whose soldiers suffered terrible losses in the First World War. Not included however, is the ordeal of the city in the Second World War when 'a North East coast town', to quote the media of the day, 'took another pounding'. This is the way that Kingston upon Hull was described; it was not named like London or Coventry, even though its brave citizens endured the nightmare of the blitz which reduced the city to ruins. The reason for this omission is that the authors consider a whole book needs to be devoted to this chapter in Hull's glorious history, not just a couple of pictures with captions which cannot in any way convey the suffering and the heroic stocism with which the people of the city faced up to their ordeal.

Kingston upon Hull has been most fortunate over the years to have been blessed by a number of philanthropists who have generously given their support in the form of gifts of land and money to provide amenities for the public in all walks of life, including libraries, public baths, facilities for education, not to mention beautiful parks and that jewel in a sylvan setting, Garden Village.

The concept of Garden Village was propounded by the highly respected businessman and philanthropist Sir James Reckitt, who said in a letter to his good friend and fellow philanthropist, Mr Thomas R. Ferens, dated February 1907, 'Whilst I and my family are living in beautiful houses, surrounded by lovely gardens and fine scenery, the work people we employ are, many of them, living in squalor, and all of them without gardens in narrow streeets and alleys. It seems to me the time has come, whether alone, or in conjunction with some members of the Board, to establish a Garden Village, within a reasonable distance of our works. So that those who are wishful might have the opportunity of living in a better house, with a garden, for the same rent that they pay now for a house in Hull, with the advantage of fresher air and such clubs and outdoor amusements as are usually found in rural surroundings.' This far sighted scheme was indeed begun and an official opening of Garden Village took place in 1908. As well as some six hundred houses there was also a club house, village hall and three well appointed blocks of almshouses.

No account of life in this bustling port would be complete without mention of the docks and fishing industry which have played a major part in the prosperity of the city. Although the docks are almost redundant, the trawlers have sadly departed and the unique community of Hessle Road has been dispersed onto the council estates to make room for development, the port of Hull will long be remembered for the importing of timber, seeds for the crushing mills and as the country's premier fishing port.

Another feature, on the lighter side of life in the city, is the Hull Fair which is eagerly awaited by many people of all ages. This, the biggest fair in the country, traditionally takes place around the first week in October and is currently held on the Walton Street site. Although the entertainments may have changed from some of those offered earlier in the century, the atmosphere and unique smell still pervade; old favourites such as the Helter Skelter, Cakewalk, Big Wheel and the Dodgems make regular appearances as do the countless and ubiquitous side stalls with their bright lights and gaudy prizes.

Kingston upon Hull is constantly changing and many of the things documented as part of a way of life have now sadly gone. Some of the older generation speak with regret of what they felt were permanent things in life, things which many feel they have now lost. It is true to say that the city has literally Phoenix-like been re-born from the devastation of the blitz and, of necessity, changes have been inevitable. Much more recent developments such as the Prospect Centre and Prince's Quay shopping malls have added to the popular and largely pedestrianised city centre.

Some things have been preserved. The Town Docks Museum in the city square is highly rated, as is the house in the High Street of the celebrated slave emancipator William Wilberforce, for many years a museum. The Art Gallery, also in the city square, boasts a fine collection of paintings and sculpture. Alas, many of the cinemas have been transformed into other utilities and, for a city the size of Hull, there are few such facilities.

The city has a unique flavour. Perhaps this is because it has always been 'at the end of the line', as the railway stops here. This factor has largely contributed to the fact that Hullensians are a unique breed. They have a reputation for being fiercely independent and a little wary of strangers. Their laconic sense of humour is in a vein of its own; some great comic actors and comedians hail from the city.

The manner of speech of those born in Kingston upon Hull is also unique, and not of the accepted Yorkshire idiom. Indeed, people do not recognise Hull citizens on holiday as being from Yorkshire. The Hull dialect has flat, drawn-out vowels. 'Five' and 'nine' become 'farve' and 'narne' and an old gentleman with a bald head, suffering from the cold would be described simply as 'owled, bowled and cowled' (rhyming with 'owl'). Though basically in the Holderness region of East Yorkshire, the Hull speech differs considerably from that in villages just a few miles away.

The city and its people have, over the centuries, made a sizeable contribution to the prosperity of this nation in several ways. They are a very proud community who make their own friendships and are galvanised together in times of local tragedy, trawling being one of the most dangerous ways of earning a living has taken a tragic toll of the city's sons. Yet if Hullensians take a liking to a stranger who makes his home among them, they are true friends indeed.

The authors acknowledge that their portrayal of life in the city may for some readers contain omissions, but they have chosen the aspects which appear to them to have most significance in conveying the pervading conditions which have made Kingston upon Hull the fine city it is today.

One

The City

Hull has long been an important British port with trading links to the continent of Europe dating back to the early medieval period. It was once one of the country's premier ports for the export of wool. The whaling industry, dating back to the sixteenth century, made the name of Hull synonymous with that now almost defunct trade. In place of whaling, a thriving fishing industry developed which sadly today is almost non-existent. The ten docks, which originally made up the city's vast complex, imported every conceivable commodity, primarily timber, seeds for the oil crushing mills and wine. This aerial view is of the Prince's and Humber Docks.

The Old Watergate was part of a building at the east end of Little Humber Street. It is thought that this alley formed the entrance to the town from the water side. Old plans of Hull show a jetty and when South End Graving Dock was made in 1834, the old landing stairs were found joining the narrow passage.

Prospect Street runs from the corner of Savile Street to join Ferensway at the Spring Bank and Beverley Road junction. It was the main route out of Hull to Beverley. Very little of the original street can be seen today as the area was heavily developed in post-war years. The original old Hull Royal Infirmary was on Prospect Street but was demolished in 1973 to make way for a shopping complex. This is an interesting view from around 1901, with not a vehicle in sight; there are only pedestrians, cyclists and the ubiquitous delivery horses.

In this view we have the tram with its letter 'B' indicating Beverley Road. Again, cyclists and the odd delivery horse can be seen. The shops are an interesting aspect of this card, particularly the shop on the second from the right. The proprietor's name is Robinson and his fascia board offers travelling trunks and Gladstone bags for sale.

Victoria Square is dominated by the imposing statue of the monarch from which the name is derived. At a later date, public lavatories were constructed beneath the statue, which stands thirty-five feet high and was sculpted by H.C. Fehr. It was unveiled on 12 May 1903 by the Prince of Wales. The building to the right with the domed roof is the Dock Offices, which now holds the Town Docks Museum with its impressive collection of whaling relics. Hull was once the premier whaling port in the country.

The domes on the building are part of that fine Italianate structure in the city centre, the Dock Offices. Designed by C.G. Wray of London, it was built between 1867 and 1871. The building now houses the city's fine collection of maritime heritage and the Whaling Museum.

Carr Lane runs parallel to Paragon Street, joining Anlaby Road and Alfred Gelder Street. Here we have the contrast of the horse-delivery carts and a tram bearing the letter 'A', which signifies it is travelling towards Anlaby Road. The name is thought to relate to the fact that it led to wet bog lands, which often suffered severe flooding to the west of Hull, 'carr' being derived from the Old Norse for marsh.

The School of Art opened in 1861. Its purpose was to teach applied art and industrial design. This was applauded by local manufacturers who saw the potential of such courses and gave it their backing. The new building on Anlaby Road, seen above, was opened in 1905 when greater space was needed. It was designed by Lanchester, Stewert and Richards. Beginning with 128 day, and 94 evening students, by 1911 the numbers had grown to 189 full time, and 251 part time students, all of whom were taught by six teachers. A varied curriculum was offered by these six stalwarts. Over the years the college prospered and offered excellent design facilities.

King Edward Street was named for Edward VII. The town centre changed considerably at the beginning of this century with the building of Victoria Square and the erection of the monument to Queen Victoria. Originally it was intended that Prospect Street should be part of King Edward Street, but objections were so strong that it was allowed to keep its name. Interesting features here are Brown's Library and also, to the right of the photograph, the man with the three-wheel delivery bicycle.

Francis Street runs between Caroline Street and Charles Street. It was built by George Pryme who was the MP for Cambridge (1832-41) and named after his grandfather, Francis Pryme, who was sheriff and mayor of Hull in the latter part of the eighteenth century. He is buried in the family vault at North Ferriby.

New Law Courts, Hull.

The Guildhall and the new Law Courts were built between 1907 and 1916. The building was designed by Sir Edwin Cooper in the Renaissance style. The large sculpture above the Law Courts bears the title *Maritime Prowess* and shows Aphrodite rising from the waves between two spirited horses. It was the work of A.H. Hodge.

PARAGON SQUARE, HULL

Paragon Square with the Cenotaph and the Soldiers' Memorial, seen here before the advent of the Second World War, which dramatically altered the city centre through air raids. The building to the left is Hammonds' Department Store. The family business was opened in 1821 and the name Hammonds became a household word in the city, so diverse was the range of goods stocked. Sadly, this building was destroyed by enemy action during the Second World War, but a new Hammonds was built and celebrated its 150th Anniversary in 1971.

A lively scene around the turn of the century. Market Place was, at one period, the point where horse drawn carriers' carts from the local villages arrived with their wares and from which they departed on completion of their business. The gilded statue of King 'Billy' presided over the scene and the gentlemens' toilets beneath the statue are just visible. They were the epitome of what a Victorian gentlemens' lavatory should be. There was a uniformed attendant who furnished soap and crisp white towels for the customers' ablutions. The interior surroundings are most impressive: the woodwork is Russian teak and the gleaming brasswork sparkles in the natural daylight that shines through the frosted glass skylight. It was a popular belief that the glass cistern once contained goldfish; indeed, some older gentlemen swear to having seen them in their youth, but it is widely accepted that this story is apocryphal.

King 'Billy', or to give him his full title, King William III, sits astride his gilded mount in the Market Place and is probably the most popular statue in the city. The statue was erected in December 1734, having been designed and made by the sculptor Scheemakers. It was paid for by public subscription, the cost being in the region of £900. It is recorded that there were 133 donors who were all invited to the unveiling ceremony on 4 December 1734. An iron railing was placed around the statue to protect it but this proved impractical, so in 1744 it was removed. Periodically the effigy is re-gilded with gold leaf so as to preserve the image. There is a story which has entered the realms of urban folklore stating that when the sculptor realized the rider had no stirrups, he drowned himself by jumping off the pier. This is totally untrue, firstly because the rider is clad in the garb of a Roman General and the Romans did not use stirrups. Secondly, Scheemakers died peacefully in 1781 at the ripe old age of 90. There is another charming story told to countless Hull children, the authors included, that when the clock on nearby Holy Trinity church strikes midnight, he climbs down from his horse.

The statue of Andrew Marvell, the poet, originally stood at the junction of George Street and Jameson Street. The statue was given to the city of Hull by Councillor John Winship in 1866 and stood in the Town Hall until it was moved outdoors in 1902. As traffic increased along George Street the statue was moved in 1922 to the top of Bond Street. In the 1960s, when Bond Street was being widened, poor old Andrew Marvell had to move again. This caused some controversy and various sites were suggested. One group thought that as he was an old boy of the Grammar School he should go back there. This idea finally won the day and in September 1963 Andrew Marvell returned to his old school. This strangely fulfilled a promise made by Alderman Benno Pearlman in 1933 when he spoke at the laying of the foundation stone of the New Grammar School.

Jameson Street, Hull.

One of the main junctions in the city centre is that of Jameson Street and King Edward Street, which was built around 1899. The statue on the small island is that of William de la Pole. It was moved from this site in 1922.

The Wilberforce Monument was erected as a tribute to a man who is still regarded by many as one of Hull's greatest citizens. William Wilberforce (1759-1833) was born in High Street at the house of his father and grandfather. At the age of twenty-one he was elected Member of Parliament for the city, where he is mainly remembered for his devotion to the abolition of slavery. After his death his body was interred in Westminster Abbey but this monument, situated between Prince's Dock and Queen's Dock, was his memorial to the people of Hull.

The first stone of the ninety foot column was laid on 1 August 1834 and in November of that year, the twelve foot figure was placed on the summit. As traffic gradually increased over the years, it was decided to move the monument and in 1935 it was moved to the site it still occupies at the east end of Queen's Gardens, but now on a college forecourt. These gardens are one of the city's real assets, providing a beautiful haven of colour and tranquility in the centre, where shoppers and workers alike can relax and perhaps enjoy a packed lunch.

A ferry sevice between Hull and Barton on the Lincolnshire side of the River Humber was first established in 1315 by a grant of King Edward II. The New Holland ferry, which began in the 1820s, was joined to the mainland by a platform. In 1877 it was replaced by a pontoon and the pier became the Victoria Pier. The landing stage which is presently part of the pier, was erected between 1934 and 1936. The paddle steamers were very popular; some people liked to use them purely for a pleasure ride, not disembarking at New Holland. They also served the practical purpose of transporting vans and cars across the river. With the opening of the Humber Bridge, the ferries were sadly discontinued and the boats sold to be used for ther purposes, one being turned into a nightclub.

A pleasant view of Victoria Pier; as with many parts of the city, the trees enhance the area. There is a mixed array of traffic, cars, a heavily loaded lorry and the popular horse drawn drays. The covered ferry-landing walkway can be seen at the top of the photograph.

Victoria Pier, Hull

Photo by F. Frith & Co., Reigate.

The pier, with its covered walkway, was not only a place to relax and take the air, but also a very busy commercial facility.

THE HORSE WASH
VICTORIA PIER, HULL

A cobbled incline runs down the side of the pier and into the river. This unusual feature is the 'Horse Wash' and was for many years used regularly by the rully and cart operators for washing down their horses and cleaning their legs and feet.

The pier proved a popular meeting place where people of all ages could perambulate or simply sit, or lounge around, and survey the river-borne traffic going about its business. On the right, this scene has been satirized by a cartoonist working for the *Hull Times* in 1899.

Whitefriargate takes its name from the white robed Carmelites who built their friary on what is now the south side of the street. When, in 1829-30, foundations for the bank building were being dug on the site of what is now Woolworths store, bones and teeth were found which were thought to be those of the friars. These were interred in the vault of St Charles' church. This busy scene, complete with delivery horses and shoppers, was photographed around the early years of this century.

This view of Whitefriargate, looking towards the town centre, is of a much later period and shows Woolworths store. The scene, reminiscent of many such busy thoroughfares, has changed little. The road however, has been laid out with brick setts and seats and is now a pedestrian area.

An early picture of Buckingham Street which runs off Holderness Road. In 1882 a Board School was built. There was much talk of naming it after Thomas Stratten, but this name was given to another school so it was simply named after the street, much to the delight of the residents. Over the years the school has changed in many ways due to the different demands of education, and in 1988 it became Buckingham Street Primary School for five to eleven year olds.

William Jackson (1828-1912) was the son of an Elstronwick farmer. He opened his first shop in Hull in 1851 at No. 28 Scale Lane, where he carried on the business of grocer and tea dealer. His business flourished and a further shop was opened in Carr Lane in 1861. By the time the above 'East Park' branch was opened in 1912 on the corner of Southcoates Avenue and Holderness Road, there were several shops in the town. Mr G.H. Bompy Hall was the first manager of this branch and stayed with the company until his death in 1950. Jacksons is still a thriving family business, its name becoming a household word in Hull over the years as it expanded.

The City Hospital was built on Hedon Road in 1885. It was more usually referred to as the Sanitorium because it was used to accommodate patients suffering from infectious diseases. The City Hospital was moved to Cottingham in 1928 and was renamed Castle Hill Hospital. In 1929 the premises on Hedon Road which had been vacated became the Maternity Hospital, which is still in use for that purpose.

These nurses, who were serving in 1917 at the Hull City Hospital for Infectious Diseases on Hedon Road, posed between duties for the camera.

The foundation stone for the Hedon Road Gaol was laid on a 12 acre site in 1865. The red brick building with stone facing was designed by the Borough Surveyor David Thorp, who sadly died in 1865 and did not see his finished building. The prison was not completed until 1870. There were 304 certified cells, 84 non-certified, 11 punishment and 24 reception cells. At the time of its opening it averaged around 200 inmates. The gaol was transferred to the Prison Commission under the 1872 Prisons Act, and in 1880, 120 new cells were added. The prison had a good health record until a smallpox epidemic hit Hull in 1900 and the infection spread to the prison. A mortuary had been added in 1890 and a chapel had been included in the original building. Employment and education, which included lessons in literacy, were part of the prison routine. A Borstal system was used at the prison from 1906 with encouraging results. It suffered severe damage during the Hull blitz of the Second World War but was re-opened in 1949 as a closed Borstal. The prison has for some years been used as a maximum security establishment which houses serious offenders and long term prisoners.

Linneaus Street takes its name from the Swedish botanist Carl Linneaus (1707-78). The reason for this is that Kingston upon Hull's first Botanic Gardens were situated on Anlaby Road from 1812-1880 and the name commemorates the gardens. From 1880 to 1893 the new Botanic Gardens occupied what is now the site of Hymers College.

Boulevard dates back to the 1870s. As the name suggests, it has the style of the French boulevards with their trees and wide roads. At the time that the development was built, the name was fashionable with the English upper and middle classes, perhaps because it enhanced their social status to be familiar with all things French.

32

In the period between 1830 and the 1860s new suburbs were developing around Hull. One such was Dairycoates, which many people considered to be an extension of Hessle Road. When the Parliamentary Borough was revised, Dairycoates was included and in 1882, it was taken into the Municipal Borough. The above view dates from the early years of this century and shows an intriguing advertising hoarding as well as one or two shops and the ever-patient delivery horse.

Gipsyville takes its name from Gipsy Black Lead, a product of Hargreaves Brothers and Company Limited of King Street. The company decided to build a model factory with houses for their workers, a practice which had become popular with some of the more enlightened employers around the country. They purchased a ten acre site on the outskirts of Hull. The name they chose was Gipsyville and by the 1920s, the whole of the burgeoning residential area surrounding it was referred to by that name.

In 1922 the local philanthropist, Thomas R. Ferens, presented eighteen and a half acres of land on Cottingham Road to the city. This was the site on which the University College was established in 1927. Once again, this generous benefactor gave practical help in the form of a gift of £250,000 in Reckitt shares to be used for the college. His fine example was followed by his friend, G.E. Grant, who in 1930 bequeathed £100,000 to the college. The first Chairman of the Council was the Revd Malet Lambert and when the college opened on 11 October 1928, there were thirty-five full time students. The first Principal was A.E. Morgan. Over the years the University has grown in size and encompasses a wide range of courses. It now has a reputation as an excellent seat of learning.

Sailor's Orphan Homes, Newland, Hull.

The Port of Hull Society for the Religious Instruction of Seamen was founded in 1821. It comprised the caring body of people who were responsible for establishing the Sailors' Orphan Homes on Cottingham Road which were usually referred to as Newland Homes. The first two houses built on the site were opened in 1895; there were eventually eight homes. In 1950 the Port of Hull Society's Sailors' Orphan Homes was renamed the Sailors' Childrens' Society.

Beverley Road Baths was built in 1905. This was some five years after the Holderness Road Baths had been built. The facilities offered by these amenities were very much appreciated by families in their areas. Not only did they offer the pleasure of recreational swimming, but also slipper baths. As most people had no other bathing facilities than the old tin bath in front of the fire, this new amenity proved most popular.

Hutt Street took its name from William Hutt who was the Liberal MP for Hull between 1832 and 1841. He was married to the Dowager Countess of Strathmore, who had originally employed him as tutor to her son John Bowes, who later founded the Bowes Museum. Hutt Street was built around 1850, a street of good, solid Victorian houses. It was part of the Hull and East Riding Freehold Land Society, with the idea of obtaining votes for the Liberal candidates.

The gracious aspect of Park Street, as seen above, at the turn of the century, was a far cry from the lane which originally connected Anlaby Road to Spring Bank. It was known variously as Cut Throat Lane, Pest House Lane and Dog Kennel Lane. From being a notorious alley down which it was inadvisable to walk after dark, it became a well-lit street with elegant houses and gardens. The transformation is said to be the work of Councillor John Middleton.

Princes Avenue was the first of the wide, boulevard-type roads on the Westbourne Estate and was officially opened on 29 March 1875. It was, and still is, a broad, tree-lined thoroughfare with desirable residences – a far cry from its original state before D.P. Garbutt incorporated it in his Avenues Scheme. It had been known for some years as Mucky Peg Lane due to its muddy state, particularly during the winter months, and anyone traversing the area at this time would inevitably end up with mud-caked footwear. At the north end are the Avenues; these tree-lined avenues of desirable residences are Victoria, Park, Westbourne and Marlborough Avenues. To the east is Pearson Park, once designated The Peoples' Park.

Spring Bank was originally the route by which Hull's water supply came into the town from Julian Springs via an open ditch down a country lane. By the 1880s it had begun to develop into a road with lime trees providing a pleasant aspect. The above scene was snapped around 1905.

Spring Bank railway crossing, leading into Botanic Gardens Railway Station which was on the corner of Spring Bank and Princes Avenue. This was a well used station until Dr Beeching decided to rob Britain of many of its rural services.

This pinnacle from Holy Trinity church was brought down during a Zeppelin raid on the city in 1915. The pinnacle, which rested in a private garden, was eventually returned to the church whilst undergoing restoration.

After the Zeppelin raid on the city on 5 March 1916, local indignation was strong and questions were asked: why was the Zeppelin allowed to bomb at leisure, using searchlights to aid the bomb drop? Why was no aeroplane sent up? Strong representations were made to the authorities in London by both the Mayor and Lord Lieutenant. An eye witness tells how the Zeppelin hovered overhead for one hour with no signs of any air defence. The two main targets on this occasion were Paragon Station and Queen Street, shown above, where the extent of the devastation is only too obvious.

Two

Sport

In 1279 King Edward I granted a licence for Adam de Everingham to hunt the chases and forests of Holderness, but it was not until the nineteenth century that the hunt really prospered. Over the years, many illustrious Yorkshire families have been represented at the hunt and Arthur Wilson of Tranby Croft, was made master of the Holderness Hunt in 1878, a term which lasted twenty-seven years. Here the Holderness Hounds are being taken across the River Hull at Wawne Ferry. Wawne, or Wagene, was a well known feature of the countryside in the days of the Domesday Book; while for many years it was thought of as an outer suburb of Hull, it was not until 1967 that it officially entered the city boundary.

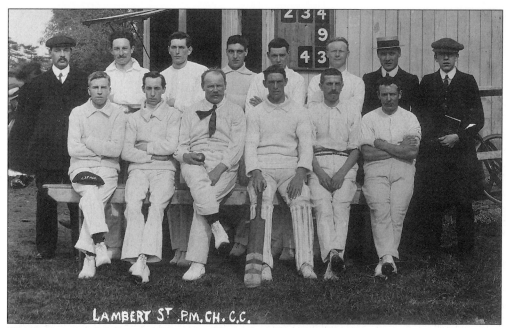

LAMBERT ST. P.M. CH. C.C.

The George Lamb Memorial Primitive Methodist Chapel on Lambert Street was built in 1894 by Thompson and Gelder. More usually referred to as Lambert Street Chapel, it has always been an active chapel offering various leisure pursuits. Above are members of the cricket team, pictured with some officials.

Many companies catered for the recreation of their employees; Hull Tramway was no exception. Apart from their cricket team they also had a tug of war team, football team, swimming team and of course, a band. There is also record of a surprising interest which brought trophies to its exponents, that of hyacinth growing.

Sport of a later period. This smiling group are the gentlemen who comprised the Riley's Snooker Team 1944-45. In spite of the great adversity suffered by the citizens of Kingston upon Hull during the early 1940s, the people tried to make life as normal as possible and many groups were formed, often representing a place of work or club, or simply for companionship and covering a diversity of interests.

Hull before the Second World War was renowned as a centre of excellence for baseball, with a number of top class teams. Here, in one of the parks, a few youngsters get together for an impromptu session. Note the pitcher with traditional baseball cap, knee breeches and leather catcher's mitt.

On 27 July 1908 a huge gathering of people waited patiently outside Paragon Railway Station to welcome their sporting hero. The man in question was Con O'Kelly, the new Olympic Heavyweight Wrestling Champion who had just won a Gold Medal in London by defeating the celebrated Norwegian wrestler Jacob Gunderson in the final. Con (George Cornelius) O'Kelly was not a Hull man by birth but by adoption; he was born in 1886 in County Cork, Ireland. Coming to Hull in search of work he joined the police force and was seconded to the fire brigade. A keen sportsman, Con, who stood some six feet three inches and was massively built, was proficient in wrestling, boxing and cycling. He joined the Hull Amateur Wrestling Club and later became British Amateur Heavywight Champion. He lost the title to London policeman Edmond Barrett after he had suffered severe back injuries when a wall fell on him whilst he was engaged in fighting a fire with his colleagues. As a result of his Olympic success, Con decided to turn professional but was defeated in his first contest by John Lemm. Undeterred, he then met the renowned strongman and wrestler Eugene Sandow, and the incredible 'Russian Lion' Georges Hackenschmidt. In 1910 Con crossed the Atlantic to try his luck on the American mat circuit. Having successfully boxed in England however, he was persuaded to don the gloves instead, under the management of former Lightwieght Champion Tommy Ryan. He began on a high note, winning his first fights convincingly. His only defeat in America was at the hands of Hank Griffin, though Con did knock him out in the return match. After a total of twelve fights and feeling homesick, Con decided to return home where he engaged in further fights with great success. He announced his retirement from boxing in 1914 and concentrated on his other occupation as pub licensee. In 1915 he resolved a lifelong ambition when he opened his own gymnasium in Freehold Street. Con O'Kelly died in 1947 at Stockport, aged 61.

Three
Parks and Garden Village

Kingston upon Hull has been most fortunate in the fact that benefactors have provided it well with parks in all areas. Each has much to offer although in layout they are all individual. They have given pleasure to both residents and visitors for many years.

Hull has long been noted for its four magnificent public parks and gardens. The four parks are Pearson Park, pictured above with the monument to its philanthropic benefactor Zachariah Pearson; West Park on Anlaby Road; East Park on Holderness Road and Pickering Park, situated on Hessle Road.

The Peoples' Park, or Pearson Park, covers an area of twenty-seven acres between Princes Avenue and Beverley Road. The land was generously donated to the people of Hull in 1860 by Zachariah Charles Pearson. This was the first public park, an amenity which was open to citizens and visitors alike, free of charge.

46

The main feature of Pearson Park was the magnificent lake which proved a popular haunt for generations of children with fishing nets. The white statue in the distance is of Queen Victoria which was carved from Carrara marble by Thomas Earle.

A view of Pearson Park which shows off the landscape to advantage, with its mature trees and colourful flowerbeds. The young lady is giving 'baby' an airing, accompanied by an older gentleman, presumably her father. To the left of the picture is the cupola from the top tower of the old Town Hall which was removed from the building when it was demolished in 1912 to make way for the present Guildhall and Law Courts.

An interesting view of the magnificent cast iron gateway leading into Pearson Park from Beverley Road; the children appear to be quite contented playing in the snow. Unfortunately much of the iron decoration was removed in later years for safety reasons.

West Park, which covers a thirty-one acre site, is situated on Anlaby Road. It was opened to the public in 1885, a main feature being the impressive tree-lined walkways.

West Park was also recognised for the elaborate and seasonally colourful floral beds which were lovingly tended by a band of dedicated gardeners.

East Park, situated along Holderness Road, is the largest of the four parks, covering an area of some fifty-two acres with formal and informal gardens, mature trees and lakes. The park was opened in 1887 and in 1913 the philanthropist Thomas Ferens presented the land which is now covered by the massive boating lake. The spectacular rock gardens were a main feature, built into the walls of which can be seen several antiquities including a Roman mosaic floor and terracotta roundels. For generations of Hull children, and the bane of many a park-keeper, this feature was known as 'Khyber Pass' and was a popular unofficial playground.

In 1913 that great city benefactor, Thomas Ferens, presented land for the boating lake, thereby considerably increasing the area of East Park. This was an amenity which was enjoyed by people of all ages as dad or grandad proudly rowed the larger boats containing mum and the kids, and younger men hired the canoes.

50

Pickering Park
HESSLE ROAD. HULL.
Opened 13th July 1911

C. PICKERING ESQ. J.P.

MRS PICKERING

THE PARK WAS
PRESENTED TO THE CITY OF HULL
BY CHRISTOPHER PICKERING ESQ. 1909.

Christopher Pickering JP was a local trawler owner and philanthropist. He generously gave land to the city in 1909 and the park which bears his name was opened on 13 July 1911. This commemorative card shows both Mr and Mrs Pickering. He also donated to the city the Museum of Fisheries and Shipping to house Hull's famous collection of whaling and similar relics. This museum was situated near the park gates and was opened by Mrs Pickering on 30 March 1912.

Pickering Park, which had a reputation for the imaginative layout of water and shrubs interspersed with ornamental flower beds, occupies a fifty acre plot on Hessle Road.

Along with other amenities provided in Pickering Park there were tennis courts. Apart from the actual pleasure of playing the game there was the pleasure of just watching play from one of the many seats provided for this purpose.

Elm Avenue, Garden Village, Hull.

Bennett's Serie
Real Photos
Copyright

Garden Village was the vision of Sir James Reckitt who believed that his employees should live in good quality housing, each with running water and modern sanitation and also a small garden in which the householder could grow fresh vegetables and fruit. The building of these houses started in 1907; they were of solid brick with external renderings of either whitewash or pebbledash in a diversity of architectural styles which makes this estate of particular interest. Typical is Elm Avenue, lined with elm trees. The sheltered walkway to the left is Lovers Walk and the avenue running at right angles is Lilac Avenue.

This singularly curious tree-lined walkway which runs from the bottom of village road, between Elm Avenue and the Oval, was affectionately known as Lovers Walk. It is said that this quarter of a mile long lane was primarily for the use of pregnant women and mothers with new babies who could exercise there in comparative privacy. Every few yards, on alternate sides, were situated wooden and wrought iron bench seats for the convenience of the ladies.

Sadly, Lovers Walk no longer caters for the young mums and mothers-to-be. The people who now mostly use it are those exercising their dogs. Many of the laurel and other shrubs which densely lined both sides of this unique feature have now gone. Even the elm trees in this view of 1970 have succumbed to the fatal Dutch Elm Disease. Part of Lovers Walk can be seen running across the bottom of the photograph with Lime Tree Avenue to the left.

The eastern boundary of Garden Village is Laburnam Avenue which is lined with London plane trees. Most of the gardens were planted with laburnam trees, but many were subsequently removed due to the seed pods being highly poisonous. The riot of yellow flowers, combined with the whitewashed walls of the houses with their red roof tiles, made Laburnam Avenue one of the most spectacular in the village during the summer months. These houses are slightly larger than most in the village and were mainly for white collar workers at Reckitts.

Garden Village, from the junction of Village Road, looking west towards Beech Avenue. The large mock-Tudor building on the left was the Manse. Many of the small saplings survive today as mature trees, their trunks so enormous one has difficulty passing them on the pavements.

Hull's famous Garden Village, which now carries a preservation order, was the brainchild of the Reckitt family. It was the vision of businessman and factory owner James Reckitt that his employees should be housed in well designed, solid brick houses with running water and modern sanitation in each home. Each was to be built with a small garden which would provide the occupant with the wherewithal to grow their own produce. After several years of planning and stages of construction, Garden Village was officially opened in 1908. One unique feature of this green and pleasant haven in the middle of a busy city is that the avenues are named after the trees which line them, such as Elm Avenue and Lime Tree Avenue. Kneeling in the middle of the road down Beech Avenue, lined with copper beech trees, are three pals, Ian Pearson, Ben Chapman and Rex Easterbrook, who spent their happy childhood days in Garden Village, with its wealth of passages and tenfoots, providing an ideal environment for three, healthy, growing lads just after the Second World War.

In July 1995 the three lads were reunited after a separation of some thirty years. In recognition of this get-together they posed for a second photograph at the identical spot in the middle of the road down Beech Avenue. From left to right: Ian Pearson of Sutton, Ben Chapman (co-author) of Withernsea and Rex Easterbrook of High Wycombe.

This view of Garden Village shows the north corner of the Oval, a large grassed area used for recreation. Some of the houses around its perimeter have small balconies from which the field activities could be observed. The street to the left leads to the eastern boundary which is Laburnam Avenue.

James Reckitt (1833-1924), who was to become a Director and Chairman of Reckitt and Sons Ltd, was created a baronet in 1894 in recognition for his stalwart services to the Hull Liberal Party. He was the youngest son of Isaac Reckitt, the founder of the company, and it was he who conceived the Garden Village scheme in 1907. James Reckitt Avenue forms the northern boundary of the village and together with Village Road and the Oval, are the only thoroughfares not named after trees.

Four
Religion

St Matthew's Anglican church, on the corner of Anlaby Road and the Boulevard, was built in 1870. The architects were Adam and Kelly. An interesting feature of this picture is the tram which bears the letter 'A' proceeding along Anlaby Road. Anlaby Road was the first thoroughfare on which the 'New Electric Trams' were introduced.

Trafalgar Street Baptist Chapel on Beverley Road was built in 1906 by the London firm of G. Barnes and Son. The Baptist Tabernacle, which was built in 1892, adjoins the church in Trafalgar Street.

Prince's Avenue and Wesleyan Chapel, Hull

The Wesleyan Chapel on Princes Avenue was built in 1905; the architects were Gelder and Kitchen. This view, taken in the 1920s, conveys the character of the avenue in its sylvan setting. The overhead lines for the trolley buses can be seen.

In the early part of the nineteenth century the number of Catholics in Hull increased rapidly. By the 1850s there were thought to be somewhere between 3,000 to 4,000, with numbers still rising. To cater for some of these worshippers St Charles Borromeo Roman Catholic church was built in Jarratt Street in 1828-9. Alterations and embellishments were added in 1894 by Smith, Brodrick and Lowther. Here is a view of the ornate altar which gives some impression of the lofty proportions of the church. Much of the ornate decoration dates from this period; some of it was created by Immenkamp, with the plasterwork carried out by George Jackson and Son, London.

St Barnabas Anglican church was situated on the corner of South Boulevard near the Fisherman's Memorial. In 1874 it was consecrated and in that same year was assigned its own district from Holy Trinity church. Built in the early English style of red brick with stone dressings, the church was designed by Samuel Musgrave and the land on which it was built was given by Henry Strickland Constable. Sadly, the church was closed in 1970 and later demolished to make way for housing. Right is a view of the beautiful altar, alas, no more. There is a certain poignancy in the demolition of some of these splendid buildings to make way for modern developments.

The St Mary's Roman Catholic School began at the Convent of Mercy on Anlaby Road in 1859. It was a kindergarten and the pupils appear to have been well catered for. There is obviously one happy little girl perched high on the magnificent rocking horse.

Endsleigh Roman Catholic Training College was established in 1905 by the Sisters of Mercy of Anlaby Road Convent in a house on Beverley Road which they had owned since 1900. A new extension was built in 1928 which meant that there was an increase in the number of students who could be catered for. The college flourished and eventually became associated with the University College Institute.

Canonesses Regular of St. Augustine - The Park - Hull.
The Convent Villa (Linden Hou
For Ladies who whish to live in the Convent Grounds.

The Canonesses of St Augustine originally came from France in 1903. In 1904 they bought Linden House, in Pearson Park, along with the land behind it in the hope of building in the future. In 1905 they purchased Willersley House from Joseph Rank and by 1906, they had built their school in Park Grove and opened it. In that year they were joined by Miss Hilda Hobson who was the first English postulant in the French convent. She took the name of Mother Philomena, worked hard as headmistress of the school and in 1920 became Mother Superior. She kept the position of headmistress until in 1972 it was found that the convent had become structurally unsafe and it was closed. Mother Philomena died in 1989 at the great age of 101, having spent her religious life at the convent.

Queen's Hall, which was designed by Alfred Gelder, followed the pattern of Central Halls which had been built in various places over the last few decades of the nineteenth century. These halls became centres of welfare and services were performed in areas rather like concert halls. A large platform replaced the more conventional pulpit and behind the massive organ were arranged tiers for the choir. Queen's Hall was built on the site of the George Yard Chapel. During the building of the hall services were held in the George Yard School, but the final services before the opening of the new Queen's Hall were held at the Alexandra Theatre in George Street. The hall was officially opened on 16 September 1905. An orchestral band gave its first public appearance on 2 December 1905. The Director of Music was Mr J. Arthur Meale, a local organist who instigated the Saturday Evening Celebrity Concerts which were enjoyed for many years. Over the years artistes such as Yehudi Menuhin, Isobel Baillie, Dennis Noble, Heddle Nash, Webster Booth and many other leading celebrities appeared there. In 1907 an organ was installed in memory of the Revd A.L. Fillingham, the first minister at Queen's Hall. He was born in 1871 and tragically, he collapsed and died whilst returning from a wedding on 4 August 1906. The hall closed in 1960 and was demolished in 1965.

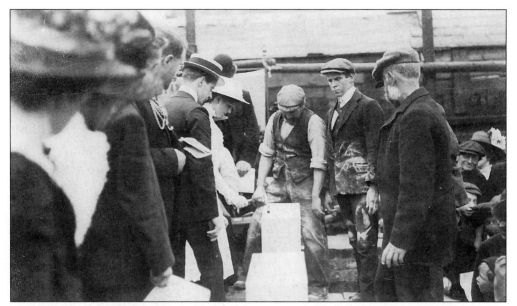

Joseph Rank was the benefactor who made Kings Hall possible. Through his generosity the property at the corner of Fountain Road and Symons Street and that adjoining Fountain Road Chapel was purchased and the existing building demolished. The foundation stone was laid on 30 June 1909.

Work is seen here progressing on the extensive building and the New Kings Hall was opened on 6 October 1910. A Methodist benefactor, Mr Henry Holloway, unlocked the door of the main hall and the minor hall was unlocked by the Right Honourable T.R. Ferens MP. The minister appointed was the Revd R.M. Kedward. He was a familiar figure in the area as he rode around the streets on his white horse. The mission was soon regularly filled for all services offered, which included not only the usual religious services, but also a Working Men's Club, rooms for reading and writing, facilities for those who had no bath at home and the free services of a lawyer, Mr F.C. Payne, who was also the organist. The hall was closed in 1968 and sadly, was demolished in 1970, presumably to make way for housing.

FISK JUBILEE TRIO.

Miss Euna M. Mocara, Mr. Eugene M. McAdoo. Miss Laura A. Carr.

Minstrel shows were very popular in the latter years of the nineteenth century, an interest which was to survive into more recent years with the *Black and White Minstrel Show*. This brought an increasing interest in black artistry. One early group who made a name for themselves were the Fisk Jubilee Trio, consisting of Miss Euna M. Mocara, Mr Eugene McAdoo and Miss Laura A. Carr. Three of the tunes they popularised were *Swing Low Sweet Chariot*, *Deep River* and *Nobody Knows the Trouble I've Seen*. It is claimed that it was through them that the true Spiritual became known and loved by the white people. They had a fantastic reception wherever they performed and it is reported that more than 10,000 people were present at an open air concert in Hull. In 1873 they appeared at Mr Spurgeon's Tabernacle. So great was their popularity that the crowd spilled onto the street and a contemporary report claims that they sang 'to a crowd that filled the street farther than the voice of either speaker or singers could be heard. Tears trickled down the cheeks of many to whom the sound of prayer or religious song was apparently unknown.'

Five

Work

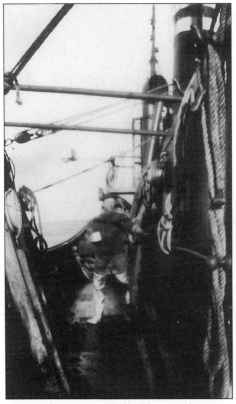

Fishing was one of the major industries in Hull. The trawlermen endured extreme hardships, often in sub-zero temperatures. They had very little opportunity to enjoy home life with their families, being away at sea for at least three weeks at a time with just a few days in home port for socialising with their friends and wives at the 'local' and treating their children. The trawlermen of Hessle Road were in a class of their own, being particularly brave, hardy and steadfast, never knowing when their trawler departed for the distant fishing grounds whether they would return home to their families.

In 1877 William and Thomas Kaye took over a saw and tool making business originally established by A. and T. Thacker. It proved a prosperous venture and over the years the name changed to T.S. Kaye and Sons. Like other works of a similar nature during the First World War, Kayes added their contribution to the war effort by grinding bayonets. The nature of the work can be clearly seen in the picture. The young man in the foreground had obviously posed for this picture. On the reverse of this card is the following inscription: 'Notice. Owing to the rapid advances in costs of all classes of Tools we regret we have to withdraw all prices. We shall be pleased to quote for any Tools on specification. T.S. Kaye & Sons. September 1915.'

Here we have a gang of Hull men doing a very unsavoury, yet essential job, which to many people would be unacceptable. They are sewer men who were responsible for inspecting the miles of tunnels which run beneath the streets of the city, along with all the obnoxious contents, including rats, about which many tales are told, not least stories of animals of great size. There was also the added hazard of contracting Wiell's disease if open cuts were not adequately protected. Note the thick boots worn by the men for obvious reasons and the inspection lamps. This is just one small group of unsung heroes who toiled in a very insanitary environment for the good of the city and its people.

Unrest was growing among local railway men and at a mass meeting on 2 February 1911, it was decided that a strike should be called in support of six fish porters and four casual workers at Paragon Station. This was begun on Friday 4 February. There was a picket line organised which was very orderly. Those wishing to cross after discussion were allowed to do so. At 10.30 pm the locomotive men joined the strike. On Saturday, officials and clerks were used to crew engines. The strike lasted three days and ended in a promise that all those dismissed should be reinstated. On 16 August 1911 a national rail strike was called; work was not resumed until 24 August. The strike was unanimous in the area and as a result of this, goods traffic in Hull was suspended. For the first time in thirty-five years the mail failed to arrive. On 19 August armed forces were drafted into Hull to guard railway property, the ferry and the pier. They were men of the 6th Infantry Brigade. Among the terms of settlement were a guarantee against victimisation and discussions of pay, which had been a bone of contention for a number of years.

The platelayers were very important for the efficient running of the railways. The coach is that of the North Eastern Railway Engineers, based at Hull. The gang of platelayers ranged in the front with some of their hand tools, was photographed around 1920.

Anlaby Road was the first thoroughfare on which the 'New Electric Trams' ran in 1889 when the privately owned Hull Street Tramways was taken over by Hull Corporation and became a municipal undertaking. The last tram made its journey through crowded streets in 1945 when the trolley buses were the Corporation Transport. The advantage these had over the trams was that they did not run on rails and were therefore slightly more flexible, though there was still some restriction due to the roof booms connected to the overhead power lines. The first trolley buses appeared on the scene in Hull in 1937. A fleet of twenty-six was set up to gradually replace the trams. The first service to be installed was from the city to Chanterlands Avenue via Spring Bank West. The last trolley bus to enter service was on the Hessle Road route in July 1945. Despite the booms having to be manually replaced on the wires from time to time by the conductor using a long pole, they continued to give service all through the Second World War and into 1961, when the first trolley bus service was withdrawn to make way for the more flexible motor bus. By 1964 they had all been replaced. There have been many generations of Hull Corporation Transport Staff; here we have a group of four in the smart uniforms which have always been part of their image.

In the early part of the century the cobbler shop was usually kept by a bootmaker who actually, as the name implies, made boots to measure. Boot and shoe repairs were also carried out and often a special polish made by the proprieter was for sale. Here we see Mr and Mrs May with their eldest son; the family lived above the shop in Hawthorne Avenue.

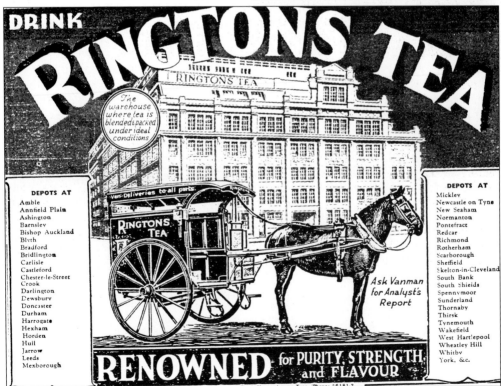

A familiar sight on the streets of the city were the horse drawn delivery vans for the Ringtons Tea company. The above advertisement from earlier this century lists their main depots in the North of England.

Hull Brewery Company Ltd began with the John Ward Brewery which was established in 1765 in Dagger Lane. John's daughter Mary married Robert Gleadow, a shipowner and builder, and when her father died they inherited the company. Eventually it passed to their son, Robert Ward Gleadow, who took a partner, Mr W.T. Dibb, who had a family brewing business in Mill Street. In 1868, due to the expansion of business, they moved to larger premises in Silvester Street and in 1888 the Hull Brewery Company Ltd was registered. There is a continued history of expansion over the years as the company flourished. It is recorded that at one period there were seventeen delivery horses, whose magnificence attracted attention wherever they went. With the advent of motor transport they were reduced to five in later years. The horses were retired in the 1970s when the company was taken over by North Country Breweries. The company regarded the brewing of beer as more than just a profession and relied on the art of the men who worked for them to produce a thick, black, mild ale which was to the drinkers in Hull and East Yorkshire the epitome of good beer. Not everyone appreciated this black brew and the company was obliged to produce a light, mild ale for drinkers in West Yorkshire. This card was sent by a son who was staying in Hull in 1907, to his father in Derbyshire.

From as far back as the sixteenth century fruit was sold in the market, and vegetables from the seventeenth century. The original fruit market was to the north of Holy Trinity church but in 1752, fruit and vegetables were offered for sale in the area at the south end of the market. These traders, offering a diversity of wares including flowers and plants, are in the Market Hall, which was built in 1904 to accommodate such produce. The Market Hall is still partially used for the sale of fruit, vegetables meat and fish.

Opposite: For many years Hull had an annual show in East Park. This had all the characteristics of an agricultural show with attractions such as the flower and produce show, crafts, pets, trade stands and the ubiquitous beer tent. One of the popular classes was the heavy horse display; a drayman from the Hull Brewery Company puts his charge through its paces in front of an adjudicator. Rivalry between these horsemen was very keen, but always friendly, in the true tradition of the working horse men.

Reckitt and Sons Ltd was founded on 1 October 1840 by Isaac Reckitt (1792-1862). In 1938 it became Reckitt and Colman Ltd, which is a name familiar to many. The Reckitt family have always been great philanthropists. Not only did they establish Garden Village, but also gave money to provide such amenties as the James Reckitt Public Library on Holderness Road. There are many more worthy examples of their munificence throughout the city. Many of their products became household words such as Reckitt's Blue, that famous blue bag added to the rinsing water when laundering 'whites' and Brasso, whose name speaks for itself as a quality metal polish. The firm was always greatly concerned for the welfare of its employees and staff, and as a result were amply rewarded by their loyalty. The above photograph shows the staff of Reckitt and Sons Ltd with some of the family fronting the group. It was posted on 17 August 1906 which gives a clear indication of the period in which it was taken.

Fields Cafe in Hull was one of the places to see and in which to be seen. It was considered the height of gentility to take afternoon tea while listening to the harmonious tones of the 'orchestra' in the early part of this century, as seen above in 1905. Another great attraction of the Fields was the aroma of fresh coffee which pervaded the area around the cafe.

Joseph Pease established seed crushing early in the eighteenth century with a mill in Salthouse Lane. It was in the first part of the nineteenth century that the industry began to expand and soon there were numerous seed crushing mills. In 1899 six Hull firms amalgamated with eleven others to form the British Oil and Cake Mills (BOCM), a limited company whose factory in Hull was on Stoneferry Road. Kingston upon Hull has long been an important place for the import of oil seeds and in the latter part of the nineteenth century, due to the growth of pasture farming, there was a bigger demand for oil cake to feed the cattle. BOCM tried to establish a margarine factory in Hull in 1917 but after the end of the First World War, butter was once again freely available. Here we have a group of ladies who worked for BOCM around 1920.

Rishworth, Ingleby and Lofthouse's Swan Flour Mills were near Sculcoates Bridge on Cleveland Street. They have been awarded first prize for a float which features the 'man who grows the grain', a windmill sail and 'the person who bakes it'. It is thought that this display was mounted around the first decade of this century.

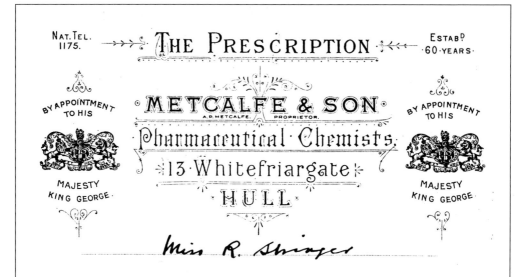

THE PRESCRIPTION

BY APPOINTMENT
TO HIS

METCALFE & SON
A. P. METCALFE.   PROPRIETOR.

Pharmaceutical Chemists,
13·Whitefriargate
·HULL·

BY APPOINTMENT
TO HIS

MAJESTY
KING GEORGE·

MAJESTY
KING GEORGE·

Miss R. Stringer

When a <u>repetition</u> of any Medicine is required, it is only necessary to <u>name the number</u>
on label.

Medicines are sent out with as little delay as is consistent with their correct preparation.
After Business Hours, and on Sundays, necessary Medicines may be obtained by ringing
the door bell, up the passage.

To prevent all possibility of errors, Bottles of a peculiar shape are used to contain remedies
for external use.

*When Medicines are
ordered to be taken by*
SPOONFULS, *a Graduated
Glass should be used to ensure
the correct dose.*

BY APPOINTMENT.

*FOREIGN PRESCRIPTIONS,
French, German, Scandina-
vian, &c., dispensed in accord-
ance with the Pharmacopœia
of the respective countries.*

This envelope contained a prescription dated 1920. Before the days of the National Health
Service all medicines had to be paid for. The doctor issued a prescription written on a sheet of
his personal stationery which was then taken to a pharmacist of the patient's choice. This was
recorded in a ledger and given a number which was written on the prescription and if further
repeats were required, each issue was noted in the ledger. The charges made would be very
modest, usually being just a few pennies, but this quite often stretched the budget of a patient
who only had a visit from the doctor if seriously ill and beyond the aid of the usual simple
household remedies.

Six

Leisure

'Walking Pictures' were very popular in the 1920s when itinerant photographers would randomly photograph people walking in the street, knowing full well very few would refuse to buy a copy of the snap. These girls were caught outside the city's Dock Offices. The practice was of necessity abandoned during the Second World War but enjoyed a brief revival in the post-war 1950s, particularly at seaside resorts.

The Palace Theatre of Varieties opened on 6 December 1897. It was designed by Frank Matcham who was responsible for most of the Moss Empire Theatres and reflected his love of the Moorish style. One of the added attractions was the use of electric lighting. The theatre held 2,000 people and had a stage which was 55 ft across and 35 ft deep. There was a performance each evening commencing at 7.00 pm with seat prices ranging from 4d (under 2p) to 2s 6d (12½p). Arrangements were made with the railway company to run a late train to Bridlington after the performance for the convenience of out of town theatregoers. On the opening night the boxes were filled by what were the described as 'The best families in Hull'. The bill on the first night featured such top class performers as Gus Elan, ventriloquist Nellie Christie and many others of note. The pit orchestra was conducted by Bob Singleton and the House Manager was Alfred Graham. The Palace, because of its popularity, outlived many of its rivals as a music hall. It was finally closed as a result of bombing by the Luftwaffe which caused severe damage to the structure during the blitz on 'a town in the North of England' in 1940.

The Royal Queen's Theatre was enormous and was said to be the largest place of entertainment in Europe in its day. In 1870 the building was condemned as unsafe. In 1871 the Imperial Hotel was built on the site of the auditorium but the stage portion was left standing and became the New Theatre Royal, which was owned by the Morton family. It was finally closed down in 1902 after the opening of the Alexandra Theatre.

With the advent of 'talkies', the cinema as a form of entertainment became increasingly popular. Most areas in the city had at least one cinema. The films were usually changed mid-week and prices of admission were very reasonable. One of the great attractions was the Saturday Matinee for children. Many stories are told of youngsters scrounging jam jars which could be returned for coppers to raise the price of admission to the 'pictures'. The Carlton on Anlaby Road was opened on 9 September 1928; it had a seating capacity of 1,671. The cinema was closed on 8 April 1967. There are many theories regarding the dramatic decline in cinema attendance during the 1950s and 1960s. They range from the advent of popular television to the boycott of British cinemas by American distributers, and perhaps, to the more mundane activity of bringing up babies after six years of war. The photograph was taken around 1930 when the cinema was in its heyday.

On 16 November 1907, a group of six African pygmies made their final stage appearance at the Albert Lecture Room in Hull prior to their departure home to the Congo, (now Zaire), after a successful tour of the music halls and theatres of Britain. The man responsible for bringing these diminutive and dusky exotics to this country was the celebrated explorer, Colonel J.J. Harrison of Brandesburton in East Yorkshire. In 1905 he brought the six Mambute pygmies from the Ituri Forest to England with the intention of showing them to the British public. The six visitors, two females and four males, did indeed prove a great success and the contemporary press sang their praises and recorded many anecdotes in their columns, including their visits to Westminster and Buckingham Palace. Their names were Bokane, Mafutiminga, Mogonga, Quarke, Matuka and Amuriape, and while in London they recorded their voices on five gramophone discs. After touring much of England and Scotland in 1905 and being viewed by an estimated one million people, they journeyed to the Continent. On returning from Berlin in 1906 they resumed their English tour. In 1907 they appeared at the Balkans Exhibition at Earl's Court in London. After their final appearance in Hull, the six visitors returned to their homes, arriving back in the Congo in January 1908.

This photograph of an important gathering of Sons of Temperance Officers was sent to their office at No. 26 Spring Street in 1905. This was the Friendly Society's Hull Office for many years. The sender of the postcard is offering portraits of individual members including Hull's Grand Scribe and also slides of the Hull Brothers wearing official gold chains, to be shown at their next Grand Division Meeting. The Sons of Temperance had a substantial following both in Hull and the surrounding areas. One of its popular benefits in the 1930s was the sick fund. For the payment of a copper a week, the member's name was put on the doctor's list and medical attention was provided by the doctor with no further charge.

The above group of Hull gentlemen belong to the National Independent Order of Oddfellows. In the early part of the century, as in most other cities of this period, Hull was well served by a large number of Friendly Societies. Many of the societies sported magnificently painted banners, often with a wealth of allegorical symbolism appertaining to thrift, industry and fellowship.

Of all the Hull shipping companies, that of Thomas Wilson Sons and Co. Ltd was perhaps the most widely known. Thomas Wilson (1792-1869) purchased a fifty ton ship in 1925 called the *Thomas and Anne*. This is thought to have been the beginning of the line. Wilson had begun his working life as apprentice to a local firm of Swedish iron importers, and soon had aspirations of forming his own company. He began trading with Sweden but soon established business with Russia, Scandanavia and the Baltic Ports. These were followed by trade with India and America. In 1916 it was thought that due to the decline in trade in the port and severe shipping losses during the first two years of the First World War, he decided to sell the company to Sir John Ellerman, and the name changed to Ellerman's Wilson Line. Like all prosperous businesses of the period, the firm had a flourishing social side including their own band, The Wilson Line Prize Band. Here we see the proud winners of the Peoples' Challenge Shield won at the Band Contest held at the Crystal Palace in 1906. On the reverse of the card is an advert for a concert given by the band in Pearson Park on Thursday 4 July 1907. The conductor was Mr A. Dennis and the programme opened with the contest march *Senator*. It was a varied programme with scope for soloists and the full band.

Many Hull firms with large work forces usually held Christmas parties for their employees' children, with food, soft drinks and games provided. Sometimes an entertainer would be engaged, a magician being the favourite, and each child would be given a present by Father Christmas in a red coat and cotton wool whiskers. The youngsters above are at the Metal Box Company Christmas Party in 1949.

Reckitt's workers had a very active social programme which included stage shows and concerts. This group in a variety of imaginative costumes were photographed in 1931.

In the 1930s, railway coaches that were considered too old for service were parked on suitable land and offered to families as cheap holiday accommodation. This coach was placed behind St Stephen's church in Hull and like the railway station, bears the name *Paragon*. The above group shows probably grandparents with their family and grandchildren, and the family dog.

Seven

Personalities

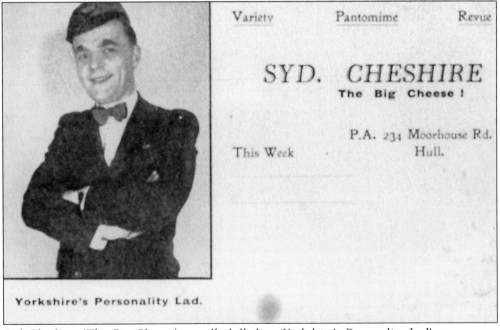

Variety   Pantomime   Revue

SYD. CHESHIRE
The Big Cheese !

This Week

P.A. 234 Moorhouse Rd.
Hull.

Yorkshire's Personality Lad.

Syd Cheshire (The Big Cheese), usually billed as 'Yorkshire's Personality Lad', was a very popular local comedian, who, as his agency card proclaims, was available for 'Variety, Pantomime and Revue'. He greatly enjoyed pantomime, making a great dame. Hull has produced some noteworthy comedians including Dick Henderson Senior, Norman Collier and comedy actors Brian Rix and Ian Carmichael. There has long been a lively club scene in the city which proved a testing ground for budding artistes. The late, and much lamented comedian Les Dawson, often related his debut in a Hull club – which did not go down well.

Before the Second World War the club scene in Hull had been strictly a 'men only' situation, but after the austerity of the war years and in a general move towards companionship, the ladies were welcomed to such social events as dances. Live music was at hand and many of the ladies were also able to show off their talents. It was only one step further to engage acts as crowd-pullers. One such act which proved very popular with the Hull clubgoers was Johnny Rix and his mother, billed as 'Mammy and Sonny Boy' – a reference to Johnny's black face make up. His mother was a remarkable lady; she had entertained the troops in the First World War and only teamed up with her son for the club circuit when she was about 60 years of age. She died in 1973 aged 78 and was on-stage entertaining just two days before her death. Johnny is still actively entertaining with a group of excellent artistes who have all passed the age of retirement. They call themselves *The Wrinklies Road Show*, play to packed houses and are always ready to appear for local charities.

86

Mr Joseph Soulsby ARCO, as his letters show, was an organist, an Associate of the Royal College of Organists. He was also the conductor of the Coltman Street Wesleyan Church Choir. This photograph was issued to publicise a concert given by the choir at Waltham Street PSE on Saturday 19 November 1904. It was a varied programme including works by Beethoven, Hadyn, Gounod and Stainer.

In the late Edwardian years and the period leading up the the First World War, Hull enjoyed the best of the music hall with many top names appearing at the local theatres. Such great performers as Gertie Gitana, Clarice Mayne (and that) Ella Shields, Hetty King, Harry Lauder and Vesta Tilley were household names. The city also had its child prodigy, a small boy called Alfie Adolfson, who lived at No. 5 Cambridge Street where Harry Lauder had theatrical digs. The great comedian took a liking to Alfie and encouraged him to perform one of his songs and part of his routine. Billed as 'Wee Alfie', he was quite a success. Lily Shaw (left) was another child prodigy who became a Hull celebrity. Her parents were the licensees of the Andrew Marvell pub in Whitefriargate. Lily was given permission by the great Vesta herself to be billed as 'Little Lily Shaw – The Pocket Vesta Tilley'. Sadly the fame of these two gifted juveniles did not last very long; they still had to attend school and became very tired and, in Alfie's case, the inevitable happened when his voice broke. Both however, felt they had enjoyed their brief success.

The film star Dorothy Mackail was born on 4 March 1903 at No. 20 Newstead Street in Hull. Dorothy was educated at Thoresby Street School and her first job on leaving was that of a shorthand typist with the *Eastern Morning News* which was situated in Whitefriargate. Her father, who was the manager of the Spring Bank branch of the Maypole Grocery, was for many years Master of Ceremonies at the Newington Dance Hall on Albert Avenue and he encouraged his daughter in her stage ambition. At fourteen she went on a two year course at the Thorne Dramatic Academy in London. Dorothy worked hard and at the end of her first year she was given a place in the chorus of *Joy Bells* at the Hippodrome, which starred George Robey. During this time she applied to the British Film Studio and successfully secured an appearance in *The Face at the Window*. The ambitious Dorothy then went on to America and earned a place in an American film *The Lotus Eaters* with John Barrymore. As the era of the silent movie came to an end with her usual aplomb she made her transition to the talkies with ease. She was not so fortunate in her personal life, making three unsuccessful marriages. The first, in 1926, was to the film director Lothar Mendes, the second, in 1931, to an orchestra leader and singer Neil Albert Millar and her last marriage, a year later, was to Harold Patterson, a New Jersy orchid grower. This marriage ended in 1938. During this period she made a number of films, appearing with such stars as Humphrey Bogart and Douglas Fairbanks Jr. Dorothy made her last film in 1937 and decided to retire to Hawaii. She did however make a few guest appearances on television, but was happy to live out her life in a suite in the Royal Hawaiian Hotel in Honolulu, where she died on 12 August 1990 at the age of 87.

A name which readily springs to mind when one considers Hull personalities is that of aviatrix Amy Johnson. Amy was born at No. 154 St Georges Road on 1 July 1903. Her father, John William Johnson, a businessman in the fishing trade, was to become her greatest supporter. Educated at Boulevard Secondary School (later Kingston High), Amy took a BA degree at Sheffield University in 1922. It was not until 1928 however that her interest in flying developed and by 1929, she had gained her pilot's 'A' licence. She also gained a ground engineer's licence in the same year. With encouragement and financial help from her father, Amy bought her first aeroplane which she called *Jason*. In May 1930, full of enthusiasm, she took off on her famous long distance flight to Australia. Not only did she win the hearts of the people of Hull, but the whole world was inspired by her courage, which culminated in a CBE in the King's Birthday Honours list. Her exploits are far too many to recount here, but her achievements were enthusiastically followed by many, including the breaking of several records. In 1932 Amy met a young aviator who had gained some recognition with a series of long flights. His name was James (Jim) Mollison. After a brief acquaintance they were married on 29 July 1932 at St George's, Hanover Square, London. They were hailed as the 'Flying Sweethearts' but unfortunately their private life was not as successful as their public image and in 1938 they were divorced. During the Second World War Amy volunteered for flying service and it was while ferrying aeroplanes for the RAF that she disappeared on 5 January 1941. Mystery has always shrouded her disappearance and in spite of numerous theories, no satisfactory explanation has yet been put forward. Her body was never found and in 1943 she was legally presumed dead.

The above mourning card was issued on the death of one of Hull's most colourful characters. John Wark Blakeney, or simply Mr Blakeney as he was affectionately known to rich and poor alike, was by his own volition the unofficial ambassador for Kingston Upon Hull. Born in 1837 he became a compass adjuster and, as he worked in a thriving port and seldom lacked jobs, he became a wealthy man. Later in life a neural degeneration which eventually led to paralysis was probably responsible for his distinctly eccentric behaviour. His usual mode of dress, except at election times, was a silk top hat, frock coat and trousers. To this frock coat he added an impressive 'buttonhole' which almost covered the entire left side of his coat front. This prodigious and highly coloured creation became his trade mark, making him instantly recognisable wherever he went. One duty as 'ambassador' from which he gained much personal pleasure, was the greeting of passengers down at the pier. He would raise his hat and welcome or bid farewell to the travellers depending on whether they were departing or arriving; he usually carried a copy of the local newspaper under his arm. He was very fond of children and would fill his pockets with sweets purchased from Ripley's on Spring Bank. These he would dole out to any youngsters he passed as he perambulated around his city. He was a very kindly man and a true Christian, suffering his debilitating illness with great fortitude until his death on 20 September 1909. A correspondent for the local paper wrote, 'The dullness of our ordinary lives will be duller than ever by the withdrawal of his cheery presence.'

Eight

In Uniform

These youngsters, who appear to be performing something in the nature of the *Anvil Chorus*, are members of a popular movement, the Life Boys. This was similar in its aims to the more popular Boy Scouts but in the Life Boys the uniform and some activities were nautical in origin, even the magnificent large brass and enamelled badge was in the form of a lifebelt. One East Hull group met regularly at the Brunswick Chapel at the Holderness end of Durham Street.

The children cared for in the Newland Sailors' Orphan Homes were given education and training to fit them for some kind of employment. Boys were obviously well instructed in seamanship but, as seen here hoeing the gardens, they also worked for the benefit of their small community. They wore traditional sailor suits and were smartly turned out.

A group of young ladies pictured with a possible benefactor, photographed outside one of the houses. Their uniforms were very neat, closely resembling the type of school uniform worn in some private schools in the 1930s. Newland Homes kept their young ladies looking right for the contemporary scene, a consideration for which they are to be commended.

Kingston upon Hull had its fair share of bands, ranging from brass to what were ambitiously called Silver Prize Bands. Some were sponsored by employers but there were also bands which were formed independently by groups of interested musicians. Here we have a local man named Harold, standing very proudly with his cornet and elaborate uniform.

The American Roller Rink on Beverley Road had a magnificent uniformed ten piece band.

The Salvation Army was founded in 1878 under the leadership of William Booth. Its basis was a Christian mission and these aims are still adhered to today. The Army has always had a large following in Hull and when Gypsy Smith visited the town on Army business it is recorded that the enthusiastic crowds almost brought the streets to a standstill. The group of workers above, both men and women, were based at the Anlaby Road Mission.

The Salvation Army was strongly family orientated. Here a proud Hull mother shows off her two sons in their Salvation Army jerseys.

This bevy of charming nurses are taking tea and relaxing in the grounds of the Hull Royal Infirmary. Sister appears to be presiding over the proceedings.

A young Hull YMCA nurse who signs herself 'Lovingly yours, Margaret 1917'. The YMCA nurses were volunteers who performed often very unpleasant duties, helping with the wounded from the battlefields during the First World War and of invaluable service during that troubled time.

Proud to serve King and Country, like many of the Hull men who joined the Hull 'Pals' battalions when the call went out for men to enlist rather than wait to be called up, this man joined the Royal Artillery.

As a port, Hull has always had strong leanings towards the Merchant Navy and the Royal Navy. The Sailors' Orphanages trained boys and fostered an interest in all matters nautical but many a boy, having once gazed upon the vessels in the docks, must have dreamed of visiting those exotic and faraway places talked about fathers, brothers and uncles. Typical of the Hull maritime tradition is this young sailor from the city aboard HMS *Leviathan*.

Nine

Events

TRIUMPHAL ARCH, WHITEFRIARGATE.
ROYAL VISIT TO HULL, MAY 12TH, 1903.

This Triumphal Arch, created on Whitefriargate for the royal visit of the Prince and Princess of Wales to Hull, was intended as a replica of the old Beverley Gate in the city.

This was the scene when King George V and Queen Mary visited the city on 26 June 1914 for the opening of the King George Dock. As we would see today, the policemen are fronting the crowds of onlookers as the party passes. The crowd contains a cross-section of the population of the city, with children at the front and all modes of dress from stylish to workaday.

There was a North Bridge built across the River Hull in the sixteenth century and as industry grew in its vicinity, a decision was taken to rebuild the bridge in 1785. Hull Corporation employed an engineer from Perth named John Gwyn. Over the years it became apparent that more bridges would be advantageous to the commerce of the city. As a result, Sculcoates Lane Bridge was the first to be completed in 1875, followed by Drypool Bridge in 1889, Scott Street Bridge in 1902 and in 1905 Stoneferry Bridge, the last of the four proposed bridges, was opened. There was a good turnout for the opening ceremony, as pictured above, with flags and bunting being hung in honour of the occasion.

The Soldiers' Memorial in Paragon Square was erected by public subscription and was unveiled on 5 November 1901. The ceremony was performed by Colonel A.V.A. Wright CB, Commander of the 15th Regimental District. The statue, which represents a soldier helping a fallen comrade, is of marble on a granite base, the rifles are bronze. It was dedicated to Hull soldiers who were killed in action in the South African War (1899-1902) or those who subsequently died from wounds or disease contracted in the course of their duties. The soldiers stand proudly to attention as a volley of rifle shots is fired over the statue in memory of the fallen. One of the tablets round the base bears the names of fifty-four men.

The poignant scene above shows the formal reception given to the victims of the *E13* submarine in Hull on 28 August 1915. On Thursday 19 August 1915 the British submarine *E13* ran aground on the Danish island of Saltholm. The submarine, while defenceless and in neutral waters, was shelled by a German torpedo boat. Fifteen of the crew were killed before a Danish torpedo boat steamed between the two vessels. The bodies of thirteen men were brought to Hull by the Danish ship *Vidar* and given full military honours by the Danes. The submarine and the rest of the crew were interned, but in November, Lieutenant Commander Layton escaped and returned to England. The bodies were taken in a funeral procession from Riverside Quay to Paragon Station. On arrival at the railway station the *Last Post* was played and a volley of shots fired over the bodies which were then placed on a train for despatch to their home towns.

Lord Nunburnholme proposed that a Hull Commercial Battalion should be raised in 1914. It was to be known as the 7th (Hull) Battalion East Yorkshire Regiment. Recruiting began at the beginning of September and enlistment was brisk. Many ploys were used to tempt the men to take the King's shilling, including marches made by already enlisted men through all the main streets of the city. The tram was an obvious attraction for the younger men, particularly when covered with patriotic and jingoistic appeals as above. There were three more 'Pals' regiments raised after the Commercials. Many of the Hull volunteers fought at Oppy Wood, near Arras in France, where a stone monument dedicated to the men of Kingston upon Hull was erected and is still visited by families of some who gave their lives there. It is said that as many as fifty per cent of the men were lost. Kingston upon Hull has also been credited with the singular honour that, considering the size of the male population, more men were lost than in any other city during the First World War.

A tram loaded with happy children has paused on Spring Bank on its way to Pearson Park. A Friendly Society called the National United Order of Free Gardeners, whose Olive Lodge met at the Reindeer Inn on Cleveland Street, decided to take all the children whose parents were members on a tour of Hull. The object was to advertise the society, particularly in the wealthier areas as they went. The treat took place on 18 August 1906; whether it was a commercial success is not recorded but the smiling faces on the trams speak for themselves.

There were memorials such as the one shown right, which was set up by the community of Ferndale, in many places around the city after the end of the First World War. The card was used in 1920 and a number of the memorials were retained for many years. They incorporated a Roll of Honour and along with the Union Jack, had mementoes relating to all the services. People who remember these memorials speak of the feeling of desolation on Armistice Day when those who gathered around them to pay their respects stood in silent tribute and recalled that dreadful sacrifice.

Like most of the other towns and cities, the citizens of Kingston upon Hull need little excuse to throw a street party or similar celebration. Shown above is just one of the many groups of ladies who organised street parties in the city in honour of the coronation of Queen Elizabeth II in 1953.

The magnificent Fairy Fountain which was erected for the big exhibition that was held in the city in November 1908.

FESTIVAL SHIP "CAMPANIA", FESTIVAL OF BRITAIN 1951.   V.7.

When the Festival ship the *Campania*, which was fitted out with displays as part of the Festival of Britain celebrations in 1951, visited Hull, many people formed long queues to board her. To many children and adults it proved to be a fantastic experience, one which one of the writers of this book still recalls with great pleasure.

Ten

Docks

On 22 July 1869 the Prince of Wales, accompanied by Princess Alexandra and a party of other dignitaries, opened the seventeen acre Albert Dock. The above photograph was published after the death of King Edward who is described as the late King in the picture. With him at the opening were the Duke of St Albans, Lady Londesborough, Princess, later Queen Alexandra and Mr Christopher Sykes, the local MP.

Albert Dock, which was sometimes referred to as the Western Dock, was once the home port of Hull's fishing fleet for around fourteen years from 1869. Above, at her berth is the Wilson Line's *Consuelo*, taken in 1921.

William Wright Dock, built in 1880, was technically a five and three-quarter extension to Albert Dock. Our view of the dock in 1905 shows both sailing ships and steam ships alongside the ubiquitous barges.

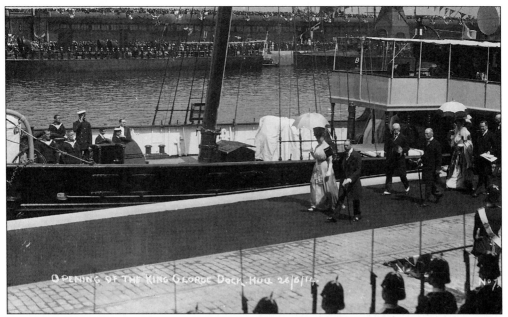

King George Dock, which was constructed on fifty-three acre site, was a joint undertaking between the Hull and Barnsley Railway and North Eastern Railway companies. Above, King George V and Queen Mary tour the complex on the official opening day of 26 June 1914.

King George Dock, which is situated on Hedon Road, was originally named Joint Dock. An extension to the dock was completed in 1969 and opened by Queen Elizabeth II, after whom it is named.

Alexandra Dock, situated on the Hedon Road, was opened in 1885 at the same time as the Hull and Barnsley Railway. It eventually covered an area of some fifty-three acres and was a principal utility for the export of British coal.

The above view of Alexandra Dock with a number of barges plying between the ships, demonstrates how busy this dock used to be. The large vessel to the right is the Hull registered ship *Torio*.

WRECK OF R.M.S. BAYARDO. JAN/12.

The RMS *Bayardo* was built by Earle's Shipbuilding and Engineering Co. Ltd of Hull and was completed in June 1911. The owners of the ship were Wilson Sons and Co., also of Hull. She was a fine ship, 331 ft long, 47 ft wide with a gross tonnage of 3,471. The vessel was only a little over six months old when on her thirteenth voyage between Gothenburg and Hull on 21 January 1912 she met her doom. The master of the *Bayardo* was Captain Soulsby and when he left Sweden on 19 January he had a crew of 44, was carrying 42 passengers and a mixed cargo of 1,800 tons. The weather was poor when the ship left Gothenburg for her home port but as she approached the Humber estuary the fog became really dense and she proceeded with extreme caution up the river towards Hull. At around 7.00 pm on Sunday 21 January she ran aground on Middle Island near the mouth of Alexandra Dock. Here she stuck firmly. The passengers, who were at breakfast, were taken off the ship in three lifeboats when the seriousness of the position was realised. Even then things did not run smoothly. They were transferred to the tug *Presto* which, in its turn, was grounded on another sandbank! In freezing cold weather the passengers had to wait a further two hours for the tug to refloat itself. Efforts to free the *Bayardo* were fruitless and as the tide ebbed, the ship began to take the strain and to break up. The fires were drawn and the captain and crew taken ashore. Weighted down by her cargo and breaking rapidly, hope of salvage was abandoned. The passengers' baggage and trunks were recovered first and a proportion of the cargo was saved, including a quantity of casks of butter. Paper and pig iron in the lower hold had sunk beyond recovery. The official enquiry found that in spite of the fact that he had taken frequent soundings, the loss was caused by default of her master and Captain Soulsby was severely censured. The court declared that he should have anchored until the fog cleared. These findings were published on 2 March 1912.

Prince's Dock, Hull.

The six acre Prince's Dock was, until 1854, called the Junction Dock. This dock encroached into the town centre with Whitefriargate to the right and the City Square with the Ferens Art Gallery and City Hall to the left. The monument to the right, which stands on Monument Bridge, commemorates the slave emancipator William Wilberforce. Beyond this the three domes of the Town Dock Offices can be clearly seen. To the extreme left can be discerned the square tower of St John's church. The magnificent sailing ship is a reminder of the days when wooden ships crammed the docks.

This view of Prince's Dock which, along with the Humber and Railway Docks were known as the Town Docks, shows steam ships of a later period.

The construction of the Ferry Boat Dock was regarded by some as another example of the Hull Corporation's failure to provide adequate accommodation for shipping. In 1801 an act was passed which authorised the enlargement of the Market Place and a street leading from it, with a proviso that a dock for ferry and market boats should be built on Crown land which was granted to the Corporation. Land had been reclaimed from the River Humber and as a result, when the dock was eventually built, it was substantially south of the intended site. The precise date is contentious, but it is said to be around 1809 when the Corporation built a timber breakwater parallel to the new shoreline and without gates at either end. The dock proved totally inadequate for the number of ferry and market boats which frequented Hull. The act of 1801 had not authorised any charges for those using the dock but boats which could not be accommodated were obliged to go to other landing stages and pay dues. The above scene shows just how busy the river was in 1903.

Victoria Dock, situated near the entrance of the River Hull was opened on 3 July 1850. The principal cargo handled was timber which provided work for the labour intensive lumber yards in the area.

THE FISH DOCK, HULL

G. 7812

Hull's fishing industry really began in the middle of the nineteenth century. The Hull Dock Company were not very sympathetic to the fishermen, giving them only restricted landing facilities. Their chance came when St Andrew's Dock was opened in 1883, solely for the use of fishermen. As the dock developed a unique community grew up on Hessle Road. It was a very close knit community with a lifestyle all its own, the dock being simply referred to as the Fish Dock. With the decline of the fishing industry in the 1970s and the break up of the Hessle Road community in the 1960s, the city lost a great part of its rich heritage. In 1988 St Andrew's Dock was filled in and the fish meal factory demolished. There is now a bowling alley and cinema on the site.

Eleven
The Dogger Bank Incident

RUSSIAN OUTRAGE ON HULL FISHING FLEET.
22.10.1904

The date 22 October 1904 perhaps means little to present generations living in Kingston upon Hull. For people living in the first decade of this century however, it was a day, to quote the words of an American President on a much later naval tragedy, 'which will live in infamy'. The event originally referred to was, of course, the Dogger Bank incident during which warships of the Russian Baltic Fleet, engaged in the Russo-Japanese War, fired on Hull trawlers mistaking them for Japanese torpedo boats. This tragedy, which caused loss of life and much damage, resulted in strained relations between Britain and Russia. Above we see an artist's impression of the tragedy.

The steam trawlers *Mino* and *Moulmein* side by side after their ordeal.

Incensed at the attack, the people of Hull gathered in large crowds at the dock to see for themselves the damage inflicted on the defenceless Gamecock Fleet by the Russian warships.

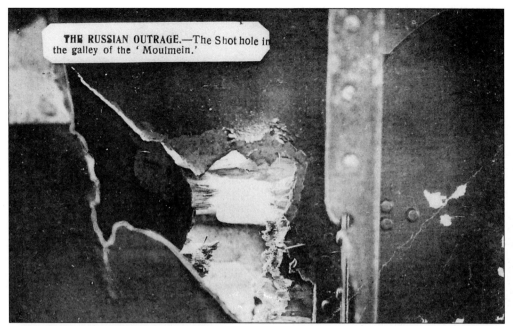

THE RUSSIAN OUTRAGE.—The Shot hole in the galley of the 'Moulmein.'

A shot hole in the galley of the *ST Moulmein* showing the extent of the damage. The trawlers were shelled constantly for twenty minutes without cease.

Steam Trawler Shot at by Russian Fleet in North Sea. Oct. 21st

A poignant reminder of the attack is the lifebelt hanging beneath shell damage on the steam trawler *ST Moulmein*.

Unaware of the impending attack by Russian warships the fishermen on the *ST Crane* were going about their lawful business of fishing when the shells rained down on them with fatal consequences.

Back in dock sightseers line the deck of the *ST Moulmein* which was one of the trawlers severely damaged in the attack. One shell passed through the galley and out the other side.

The funeral of the victims took place on 27 October 1904. The Royal Antediluvian Order of Buffaloes Band and the Salvation Army Band, whose drums were covered in black, accompanied the procession.

When all the coffins had been collected from the houses where they had rested, the funeral made its slow and solemn journey along Spring Bank past crowds who crammed the pavements as many as seven or eight deep. The bodies were interred at the Western Cemetery.

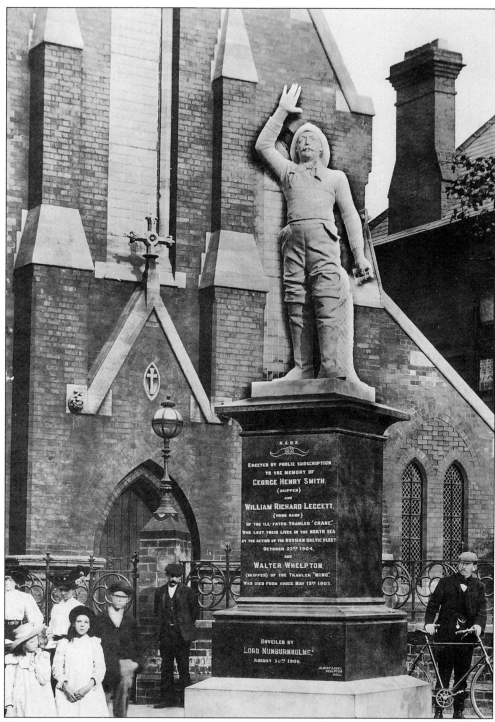

This impressive statue was erected at the Boulevard on Hessle Road and unveiled in August 1906. The memorial, capped with a figure in white Sicilian marble, commemorates the tragic incident. The fisherman portrayed is thought to be a representation of Skipper George Smith, one of the men who lost their lives.

Twelve

Hull Fair

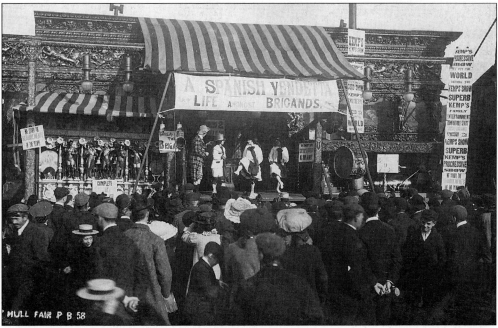

HULL FAIR P B 58

The question 'a 'yer off to fair?' was one which sprang from the lips of young and old, in and around Hull, for many generations. The fair was of course the famous Hull Fair which is allegedly the largest fair in England. Now held from around 11 October, it can trace its origins to 1278 during the reign of Edward I. The fair was first held for two weeks on the ground of Holy Trinity church, four years later however it was moved to the Market Place. During medieval times its main function was for trading purposes with a wide variety of commodities being offered for sale. It was not until the seventeenth century that the fair took on a more light hearted aspect with more entertainments being offered for the edification of the public. A horse fair was being held at Walton Street around 1887 and the Corporation decided that this six acre site, close to the North Eastern railway line, would be suitable for the fair. Hull Fair still flourishes today on the Walton Street ground, and for local youngsters is regarded as the event of the year.

Aspland and Marshall's Switchback with gondolas by Savages of Kings Lynn. A switchback was a ride comprising of cars driven around an undulating track. The scene above was taken at Hull Fair around 1904.

The Joy Wheel was a short lived phenomena. This simple attraction relied on centrifugal force and a polished wooden wheel some four feet in diameter. The object of the exercise was to see how long the riders could remain seated on the wheel as it increased in speed before depositing them among the surrounding spectators. The Joy Wheel above probably belonged to Green's and was at Hull Fair in 1910.

The proscenium of the famous Bostock and Wombwell Menagerie at Hull Fair, at which it was a popular attraction. George Wombwell (1777-1850) was one of the pioneering menagerie showmen. After his death his three menageries passed into hands of three people. Number Two, which was left to his niece, Mrs Edmonds, eventually came under the Bostock management and was itself eventually divided into three separate menageries.

This close up view of Bostock and Wombell's Menagerie, taken around 1919, shows Billy the pelican who was used as a crowd drawing attraction.

Hull Fair, like many similar fairs, was one place where persons of over-abundant proportions could exhibit themselves, thus earning a living. What other chance would a person standing 7 ft 9 in, 2 ft 6 in, or tipping the scales at over 30 stone have of normal employment? Such persons, plus medical curiosities like Siamese twins or macrocephalics, earned a good living on the fairground circuit. Two popular visitors to Hull Fair were the gigantic Australians Barney and Joy Worth who were billed as 'The World's Heaviest Married Couple'. They backed up their claim by offering money to any heavier married couple. They made their first appearance here in 1947.

The Haunted Castle was a very popular attraction. It was simply a darkened interior in which were strategically concealed such devices such as a wind machine and ghostly mechanical effects. The emphasis was on surprise and fun and at one penny admission it was a reasonably priced thrill.

Tattooing, or the practice of producing durable designs under the skin of humans with the aid of needles and pigments, is one step on from the primitive practice of body painting practised by primitive people. Tattooing was widely practised by the Ancient Egyptians and many Pacific and South Asian societies. The art form was adopted by European seamen, and in the nineteenth century both men and women were having their bodies tattooed simply to earn a living exhibiting themselves as pictorial curiosities. One such tattooed lady was Princess Christina who was presented at Hull Fair by Tom Wortley in 1912.

HULL
for the Fair

11th to 17th October

Cheap Day Return Tickets

at ordinary single fare for the return
journey will be issued to Hull (Paragon
Station) and Hull (Corporation Pier) from
all stations within a radius of 60
miles every day during the Fair

Available any Train

TICKETS CAN BE OBTAINED IN ADVANCE

Tickets, bills and all particulars can be obtained at the Stations, also at the usual Town Offices.

For further information apply to the District Passenger Managers, York, Tel 2001 (Ext. 396), and Leeds, Tel 20615.

CONDITIONS OF ISSUE OF EXCURSION TICKETS AND OTHER REDUCED FARE TICKETS

Excursion Tickets and Tickets at fares less than the ordinary fares are issued subject to the Notices and Conditions in the Company's current Time Tables. For Luggage Allowances also see Time Tables.

Children under three years of age, Free ; three years and under fourteen, Half-fares.

L·N·E·R

YORK, Sept., 1935

Herald, York—23,250

The popularity of Hull Fair can be gathered from the above LNER poster dating from 1935. The mention of Hull Corporation Pier, whose booking office was technically a railway station without trains, indicates that people travelled from the south bank of the Humber to visit the fair.

Thirteen
The R38 Disaster

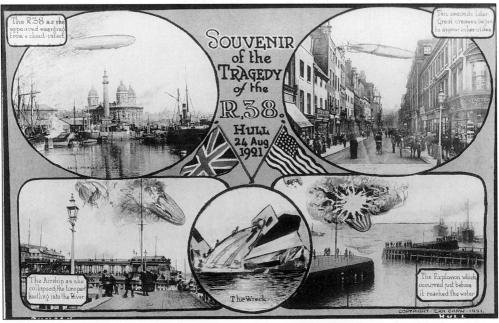

It was a warm Wednesday evening and many of the citizens of Hull were heading home from work around 5.35 pm on 21 August 1921. Hoards of people turned their eyes skywards as a long silver shape silently passed over the city centre; they marvelled at this feat of engineering as the slender airship headed towards the River Humber. Suddenly there was a terrific explosion which shattered the windows of many shops and houses, the beautiful cigar shaped craft split in two like a cracked egg, flames rapidly engulfed the stricken airship as it tumbled downwards onto the murky waters of the River Humber. Thus the R38 met its ignoble end. The R38 was at the time the biggest airship ever built. Constructed at Howden it was on trial manoeuvres before being handed over to the American Navy as the ZR2. Out of a combined compliment of forty-nine British and American personnel there were only five survivors.

No. 1.   The Wreck of the Z.R.2 at Hull, 24/8/21.   The 100 Ton Crane at Salvage Work.
W. Benton, Merchantile Chambers Hull

Much of the burned out framework of the ill fated R38 (ZR2) was salvaged. Above, this 100 ton crane lifts part of the wreckage from the River Humber.

This tangled mass of wreckage was the bulk of the remains of the ill fated airship.

The flag-draped oak casket containing the silk lined metal casket in which the embalmed bodies were taken back to America.

No 7. Funeral of some of the Victims Giant Airship Disaster At Hull Aug 24th 1921.

Walter Benton, Mercantile Chambers, Hull.

Part of the large funeral procession which passed through the city centre on its way to Chanterlands Avenue for the burial of the victims. The military funeral attracted thousands of spectators who lined the streets in dense, silent crowds. The principal mourners from the services, government and American Navy were, Lieutenant General Sir Ivor Maxse (Army Council), Captain S.H. Radcliffe (Lords Commissioners of Admiralty), Major General Sir F. Sykes (Comptroller General of Civil Aviation), Air Marshall Sir H.M. Trenchard (Chief of Air Staff), Air Vice Marshall A.V. Vyvyan (representing Secretary of State for Air) and Lieutenant Commander R.E. Byrd (U.S. Bureau of Aeronautics).

This silver, black edged 'In Memoriam' card was issued to mark the tragedy. Inside were printed the names of those who perished including Air Commander E.M. Maitland CMG, DSO, AFC. It is inscribed on the inside, 'In Memory of the Officers and Men who perished in the R38 on Wednesday, August 24th 1921.'

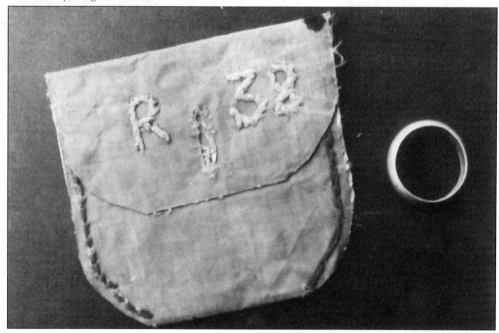

Much of the wreckage of the R38 was brought ashore where souvenir hunters both young and old acquired pieces of the dull silver coloured fabric and alloy framework. A thriving industry resulted with ash trays being commercially moulded for the Hull Brewery Company and homemade matchbox holders, paper knives, finger rings and models of the airship being produced. The small purse made from piece of the fabric and the ring, stamped R38, are in the possession of the authors.

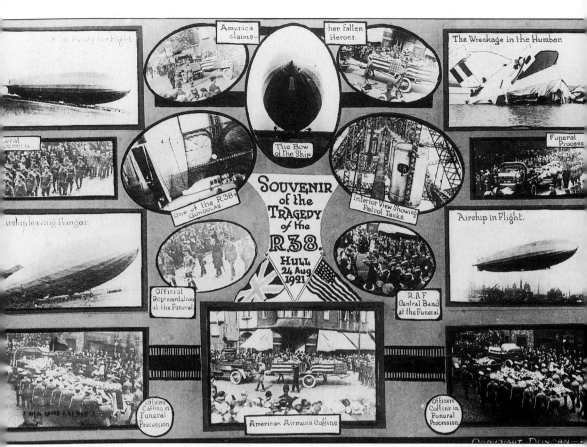

This multiview postcard is typical of the type of souvenir which followed in the wake of tragedy or national disaster. The sixteen vignettes show the R38 from leaving Howden, in flight, to the moment of tragedy and the subsequent funeral procession.

The arms of Kingston upon Hull are blazoned as follows: Azure three ducal coronets in pale or., meaning three gold open crowns placed one above the other on a blue ground. The above depiction of these ancient arms is taken from a pane of stained glass in the east window of St Mary's church, Lowgate, *c.* 1400.